Copyright © 2021 Shannon Guerra

With gratitude to the contributing authors, who each retain the copyright for their individual works.

All rights reserved. No part of this book may be reproduced in any form or by any electronic or mechanical means, including information storage and retrieval systems, without permission in writing from the publisher, except by reviewers, who may quote brief passages in a review.

ISBN 978-1-7360844-6-5

Published by Copperlight Wood
P.O. Box 870697
Wasilla, AK
99687

www.copperlightwood.com

Design by Shannon Guerra. Photography by Shannon Guerra, with the exception of page 44 by Jessica Dassow and pages 60-62 by Megan Ancheta.

Unless noted otherwise, scripture quotations are from the ESV® Bible (The Holy Bible, English Standard Version®), copyright © 2001 by Crossway, a publishing ministry of Good News Publishers. Used by permission. All rights reserved.

Portions of scripture in **bold** are the author's emphasis.

This title may be purchased in bulk for ministry or group study use. For more information, please email shop@copperlightwood.com.

Printed and bound in the USA.

contributors

MĒGAN ANCHETA
beach comber, fancy macaroon eater, owner of Allergy Free Alaska, LLC
www.allergyfreealaska.com
allergyfreealaska@gmail.com

JESSICA DASSOW
lover of old-fashioned flowers, chicken collector, avid reader of classic picture books
www.planted-by-the-river.com

CYNTHIA HELLMAN
lover of dark chocolate & fruit combinations, hard of hearing, year-round flip-flop wearer
www.cultivatedgraftings.blogspot.com

RENEE PETTY
barefoot hiker, sunset watcher, greenhouse gardener, dances in the kitchen and laughs at her own jokes

LACEY STEEL
reluctant gym goer, coffee snob, lover of talking to strangers
www.cultivaterelationships.com

contents

06
move me

10
mountain climbers and obedience

14
carrying fire

20
following instructions

24
to be truly brave

26
obedience laid bare

29
stewards of the mysteries of God

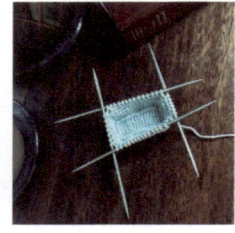
36
whatever it takes

39 little arks

40 right of way

44 in between

48 consider it an adventure

50 all it takes is doing

54 an evening prayer for bold obedience

57 apple snug

59 pumpkin spice scones with cardamom icing

62 proximity: where brokenness becomes wholeness

66 1 corinthians 15:58

68 study guide

73 notes

move me

I was up in the wee hours trying to get ahead of the day. Our baby was up and at 'em earlier than normal, playing at my feet. The computer was on, my papers were right there, the coffee was steaming, and I was ready to work.

However, three cats were also there, and I was interrupted every ninety seconds by trying to keep them away from little Finnegan's violent affection.

Except for Knightley. I didn't have to move her; she moved herself. After Finn used her tail as a leash a few days earlier, she didn't need any help staying away from him. She was highly motivated.

Sometimes we need a little motivation to move us. And I needed a little motivation that morning; I was trying to read ten pages of fine print, and I had already scanned ahead to see if there were any pictures or graphs to break it up a little. But nope, no extra white space at all, just more big words in tiny font. All the legal details about Us, Them, and the Agreement. We were in the process of revising and re-launching my first book with a publisher, and I needed the motivation of partnership and accountability.

I know me. I wanted to do this project, but I knew I would think about it off and on for a few years, feeling incompetent and not-enough about the hard parts of the process until I finally gave up on ever doing it, and felt like a loser. Big sad face. But now, with this paperwork in hand, I was highly motivated to move – not only to get it done, but to also pull other projects forward that had been simmering on the backburner.

In that season, God was talking to me a lot about cooperating with change, doing the work that needs done, and finding joy in the process. A few days earlier in the middle of the night, our squirmy nine-month-old kept waking, nursing, and sleeping in three-minute increments, and in my exhausted stupor I finally realized he was too restless to sleep because his diaper was wet. Then when I tried to change him, he fought like mad. It was like trying to put a snowsuit on a fractious baby kangaroo in the dark while you're barely conscious, with the bonus possibility of it peeing on you.

If you'd stop kicking, we could do this faster and get it over with. The second I thought it, I realized God had been telling me the same thing for who knows how long. I had my own things I was writhing and whining and trying to sleep through, ignoring the need to change.

We feel restless and edgy, but we're comfortable enough to not want to expose ourselves to something new and fresh that is better for us. **We will all be changed; how long will we waste time resisting it?**

Sometimes we'd rather wallow in fitfulness. We'd rather ignore it until it reaches the tipping point, and something motivates us to move, to get up and do the thing we've been avoiding.

Motivation is important; it's the fuel behind our choices, our work, and our change. *In Him we live and move and have our being*[1] and we are meant to live and move and be in joy, not resentment.

We don't always need more tools or help to convince us to do what needs doing. We need the want-to.

For example, if dentists really wanted us to floss, they wouldn't lecture and send us home with another packet of tooth floss destined to be used twice and then lost in a bathroom drawer. If they really wanted us to floss, they'd send us home with kettle corn and little samples of beef jerky. *That's* motivation.

We might make excuses about needing the right tools, or time, or ability to do it, but usually it's not about those things at all. If we're procrastinating, we probably already have everything we need to get what we want. We just don't want it bad enough.

It holds true even in the littlest things. I've always known that drinking plenty of water keeps us healthy, but I never drank enough of it because the reasoning was just so...vague. But then I had an emergency surgery and I learned, *Wow, water helps you keep your organs.* That's highly motivating. The stuff is not just for showering and making coffee with, who knew?

So now I often eat spicy food to motivate myself to drink more water, and I'm also constantly pushing water onto our kids. They totally love this, as you can imagine. It happens like this: Afton comes to the kitchen and asks for a drink from the fridge, and I tell him, Yes, but drink some plain water first.

He says, No thanks, he doesn't want it that bad. (That's my boy. Spitting image, sometimes.)

But then in a move of brilliance that can only be credited to a prompting of the Holy Spirit, I start eating pico de gallo. And you should probably know that Vince got tired of me eating all of the pico and made this particular batch with an extra serrano pepper and the tears of Hades. (He denied it, but I know his tricks and ways, and I persevered, anyway – two extra glasses of water down the hatch, no problem.)

This was the batch I was eating when I offered Afton a chip. And if you give an Afton a tortilla chip, he's going to want some pico to go with it.

"Whoa," he said, and coughed a little.

"Now you want some water, don't you?"

And he did. Two cups down the hatch, no problem.

God can show us how to want something badly enough if we ask Him. I think He longs to make it easier on us. Even in that hard thing that we know we need to do but we just aren't motivated enough – God knows us, He's a good father, and He knows how to give us the want-to.

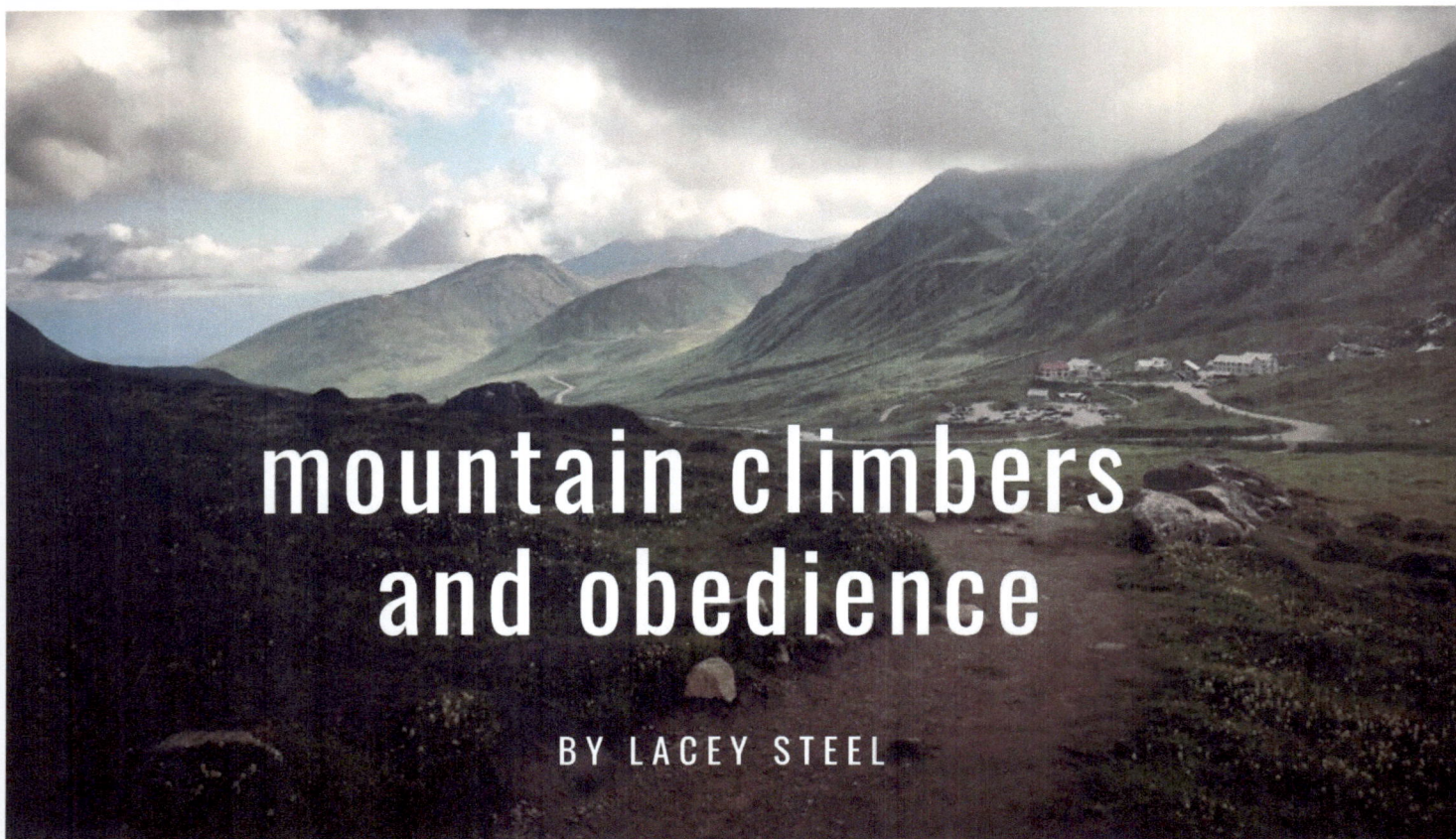

mountain climbers and obedience

BY LACEY STEEL

Years ago, I decided to get my life together and become a gym member. I felt that conquering the area of fitness was the key to me reaching my goals. My first class was advertised as *fast paced and interesting, destined to give you abs of steel and an amazing physique* for only a thirty minute commitment.

Excited, I showed up to the class ready for change, and ready for this future me.

Eventually the fitness instructor walked through the door, glassy-eyed and holding a coffee. With a casual glance to her eager students and a sip of her beverage, she demanded us to get on the floor and begin a series of "mountain climbers."

Now if you have never had the privilege of this specific workout move, let me explain it. Imagine you are climbing a mountain, but the floor is a mountain and the floor never ends and though it is a floor, it has a steep dark drop to insanity and failure as you realize you can only climb this endless mountain for maybe ten seconds.

So here I am, in class, ready to embrace my new me. The svelte future version of myself calling to me. This version is not only fit, but a morning person. She walks through a spotless home and manages to run a Fortune 500 on the weekends. Her children never argue and always respond to her requests with a smile and a happy attitude. She never has to say no to anyone or anything because she finally has it ALL together.

And the only thing standing between me and this reality is a gigantic floor mountain.

Determined, I climb away vaguely realizing that the instructor has not moved and is nonchalantly sitting cross-legged in front of us sipping her coffee and yelling her demands.

"Faster! Push!!!"

I start to hyperventilate a bit and the mental future me is slightly obscured by my frantic need for air.

"Faster! Push! FASTER!!"

A dispassionate yet angry voice yells from the front of the room. I pause and drop to my knees as my legs can no longer move. The mountain before me is too big and too intimidating to climb.

As I sit trying to breathe, I began to realize that the instructor is again yelling. But the mantra has changed.

"Get off your knees! You! You on the ground! Get up, we are not moving forward until you are moving again. We're ALL waiting on you!!!"

I slowly realize she is pointing at me. She is yelling at me. Twenty pairs of eyes sneak glances my way tensely waiting to see what is going to happen.

Now I would like to tell you that this instructor motivated me to get off the floor and hop back on the floor mountain. But in reality, she only motivated me to get off the floor and leave the class…and cancel my membership.

Obedience to her demands felt impossible. I felt angry and unseen. The determination I had felt to "push harder" was almost instantly crushed by her carelessness of my needs. I physically and mentally could not do what she wanted me to do. I would have gotten up in a minute and tried if only she had really looked at my situation and seen that I was incapable of doing what she wanted me to do. But she didn't. She didn't care.

I want you to think back to the last time God told you to do something. Or even not do something. Basically, that last time you felt like you were to obey the Father.

Did you question it? Did you hold back or procrastinate doing it? Why? Why do we do this?

I think it's because we can get this vision in our mind of God being very similar to this disconnected gym instructor.

I think that when I have a hesitancy to obey Him it's because I actually do not trust Him. If I'm honest, it's because I think He doesn't really see me, or He hasn't consciously weighed the cost of what He is asking me.

He knows me better than I know myself. He knows my concerns and my needs; He hears me and He sees me. Not only does He let me catch my breath, He breathes the very life into me that I need to be whole.

When He sees me on the floor trying to catch my breath, trying to reach these unobtainable goals, that is when He directs me. That is when He asks obedience out of me, not to overwhelm me but to change my vision – change it from something I think I want to something I actually need. Over and over again Jesus stated that He was about Joy, Wholeness, Freedom. The fact of the matter is that our own vision of perfection, our own vision of who we think we need to be, can steal these things from us.

Obedience is what saves us. It allows us to move forward to something better – something we might not even have the capacity to see. But the Father sees it. He sees us.

Our obedience allows Him to build a future for us better than our wildest dreams.

carrying fire

The Lord gave me this amazing idea, and I was so excited to follow through... that is, until it was time to actually do it.

And then, as responsible people do, I came up with a lot of good excuses.

I hadn't showered the night before. My hair was a mess and in no condition for video. I needed to think through these details and prepare some more. Suddenly, cleaning my desk was of the utmost priority, so I put away the tape and scissors, filed a few papers, and stacked the books. I even considered sweeping the floor or washing the windows. I mean, it was that bad.

Add all of this to the fact that I have the technical skills of a Chihuahua. So when the Lord asked me to start praying online with whoever would join me – which, as I type it, sounds like the easiest thing ever and nothing to be intimidated by – I had no idea how to go about it.

And then when I finally did do it, it was in two parts because I ran out of space and had to add the rest after figuring out how to splice and trim it *(blankety-blank)* to get all three minutes of video together.

Because, like a Chihuahua, I told you.

> *Until I come, devote yourself to the public reading of Scripture, to exhortation, to teaching. Do not neglect the gift you have, which was given you by prophecy when the council of elders laid their hands on you. Practice these things, immerse yourself in them, so that all may see your progress.*
> *– 1 Timothy 4:13-15*

But the opportunity to pray with and for anyone who wanted to join me on a weekly basis was a no brainer – until my brain kicked in and started making excuses for me, of course.

Isn't that the way it is with going forward, though? He calls us outside the comfort zone, but somehow we'd rather put it off or just not bother because we don't understand how much breakthrough is at stake in going there.

Too risky. Too scary. Too unfamiliar. Too unknown.

We ask Him for direction, to light our way, and often the way He does that is by lighting a fire under us. We often respond by extinguishing those fires in any number of ways instead of having the boldness to pick up the fire and carry it.

We are our very own wet blanket, smothering our own growth.

We pooh-pooh it, telling ourselves it was just a silly idea and not Him at all, when in reality these steps of obedience are the key to unlocking answers we've been searching for.

Or we put it off, and our delay, like most symptoms of laziness, makes us work harder in the long run.

And sometimes we give up before we start because it won't be perfect, and we can't control how people will respond to us. So we sacrifice our breakthrough on the altar of perfectionism and control – which is really just a monument to ourselves and our pride. If that altar were made into an idol, it would look like us.

But we often need to accelerate our pain to accelerate our progress, so we might as well jump in and start doing it, whatever it is: Making that phone call. Starting that business. Filling out the adoption paperwork. Researching that ministry opportunity. Writing that book. Going on that mission. Taking that leap.

Saying yes.

We wrestle with the feeling of exposure after being vulnerable and laying it all out there, in teaching, writing, speaking, mentoring, moving — however you are leading others as they watch you follow Jesus. Yes, there's tension. Yes, we pause and squirm.

But it turns out, the best way to get anywhere is usually forward.

Going, doing, and obeying – as opposed to stalling, fretting, and backsliding. Because life has a current to it, and every moment we are either moving further up and further in, or drifting back downstream. There is no neutral.

We need to remember there is a cost to disobedience, and it is much higher than the pain of going outside our comfort zone.

> *He drove out the man, and at the east of the garden of Eden he placed the cherubim and a flaming sword that turned every way to guard the way to the tree of life.*
>
> *– Genesis 3:24*

When we move in obedience, we go in freedom – bringing light, making progress, carrying His Presence as fire. But when we are forced to move by our own disobedience, we are pushed out, vulnerable to slavery.

The truth is, we move outside the comfort zone either way.

In that same season, I sat near the back of the auditorium during a friend's memorial service. The rows ahead of me were filled with people, some of whom I knew, but most of whom I didn't. In the middle of a song, I saw a picture in my mind of my friend watching us with her new perspective as we mourned and remembered her. And then I had a weird thought: I wondered if she could see who was really engaged in the Spirit, in worship and prayer. I wondered what it would look like.

It would look like My fire on them, Love, the Spirit said. It would look like them carrying My Presence.

> *When the day of Pentecost arrived, they were all together in one place. And suddenly there came from heaven a sound like a mighty rushing wind, and it filled the entire house where they were sitting. And divided tongues as of fire appeared to them and rested on each one of them. And they were all filled with the Holy Spirit and began to speak in other tongues as the Spirit gave them utterance.*
> *- Acts 2:1-4*

But life rarely looks the way we expect it to. Sometimes tasks (or entire seasons) are harder than we thought they would be. Breakthroughs take longer than we expect because we can't control all the outcomes. But that doesn't mean we're getting burned by carrying the fire – it usually means we're being refined by it as we are learning, growing, doing, and obeying. I'm pretty sure it usually means that we're getting it right.

The fire will move us one way or the other: We can either be driven by it under threat of burning, or we can learn to carry it where He calls us to go. **Those who carry fire do not also have to carry fear** when their obedience reflects their relationship with God.

The sinners in Zion are afraid;
   trembling has seized the godless:
"Who among us can dwell with the consuming fire?
   Who among us can dwell with everlasting burnings?"
He who walks righteously and speaks uprightly,
   who despises the gain of oppressions,
who shakes his hands, lest they hold a bribe,
   who stops his ears from hearing of bloodshed
   and shuts his eyes from looking on evil,
he will dwell on the heights;
   his place of defense will be the fortresses of rocks;
   his bread will be given him; his water will be sure.

- Isaiah 33:14-16

We can't see it now, but if we could, what would it look like on a Sunday morning in a sanctuary full of attenders at a normal church service? Out of the dozens or hundreds in the room, how many of them are praying, worshipping, in His presence, and carrying fire? What would it look like in any given home or business, during a packed gathering of friends and family, or just a normal day of laundry and school and work – as though you could look across the room and see fire above the heads of those who are abiding?

The world doesn't necessarily change if we just go to church, or gather with friends, or fill our days with our own agenda of busyness. It changes when we carry fire to the places He calls us. So, what would it look like in our normal days, going about our business, if we all moved by the light of that Fire instead of running from it or smothering it, and getting smoke in our eyes?

A flame over the mom who is uneasy about a child's behavior: She is interceding, and trusting God with the outcome.

Another flame over the man who is stressed about an upcoming meeting: He is asking God for His words and composure, and refusing to bow to the fear of man.

Flames over the students who are inundated with pressure: They are abiding, choosing to pursue God's favor instead of the favor of their peers or professors.

Peace comes from abiding, so we abide. He is so very near. Right there. With you. Close as breath.

Waiting to hear you. Waiting to be heard. Not accusing, not condemning, not repeating the tapes in your head or the things anyone said.

Ready to tell you truth and give you revelation. It comes in the waiting, in the bold approaching, confident in the Father who loves you and always tells the truth.

It comes in the heart that's willing to hear correction because it trusts the Father's discipline.

It comes to the one willing to hear His hard questions and gentle probing as He prods callouses off our hearts to find the tender, healthy tissue underneath.

It comes to the one willing to set the rush, the agenda, the production aside, to wait for His timing, direction, and voice.

He comes. He doesn't have far to go, because He's been with us all along.

His fire lights our way, and others will be able to find Him by the light of the flame we carry. We say yes, facing our fears and excuses, and we're no longer afraid of what the fire will do to us. We are invincible to burning when we learn to carry it.

following instructions

Having kids who bake is a dangerous thing. I know it sounds lovely, but there's only so much experimentation with sugar that can happen before you gain fifteen pounds, get tired of the mess, or something explodes.

Case in point: A child was making caramel sauce for an ambitious birthday cake, and it seized into toffee which turned into concrete in the bottom of my favorite cooking pot. Enter an hour of aerobic stirring while adding cream; the result was an extra two and a half cups of caramel sauce, which was *not* going to help me stay away from sugar.

So in desperation after a week of baking frenzy, I asked the kids if we could teach them to make green smoothies, or salad, or *something*, in a what-have-we-done kind of despair. And Afton, my son who makes professional-level biscotti, breads, and pizza, answered, "You can teach us, but that doesn't mean we'll make it."

Gaaahhh.

I can't be too hard on him, because I tell the Lord the same thing so often, in so many words. He says things like this:

> *Rejoice in the Lord always; again I will say, rejoice.*
> *- Philippians 4:4*

...and also, this:

> *Trust in the Lord with all your heart,*
>   *and do not lean on your own understanding.*
> *- Proverbs 3:5*

...and often, I basically respond with, "You can tell me to, but that doesn't mean I'll do it." I complicate my life by trying to do things my own way until finally going back to Him and follow His instructions that I should have just obeyed in the first place.

If the Lord has said, *Rejoice always, pray without ceasing, give thanks in all circumstances; for this is the will of God in Christ Jesus for you*[2] (and He has), then I need to do those things in order to see the breakthrough I'm waiting for.

Could it be that our breakthrough is waiting for us to rejoice in advance? Could it be that when we wait to rejoice until we feel our circumstances give us a good reason to, we delay our own breakthrough? What

might happen if instead, we followed His instructions and rejoiced at all times because He is good and we can trust Him?

We gain so much when we see with His perspective. We tend to make things so complicated, but often, He has already told us exactly what to do.

Just like we tell our kids.

In the afternoon on a fall day, our kids had been outside for all of ten minutes before they asked to come back inside. "It's *freezing*," they said.

I checked the thermometer and noticed the temperature was in the upper thirties – definitely, scientifically, *not* freezing. So being the sympathetic mom I am, I said, "No. You're Alaskan, get used to the cold again."

Five minutes later one of the kids asks again, and I reconsider. *Okay, let's make a deal.*

"You can come in early *if* you plant the garlic," I say. "This is the last day to do it before it snows, so if you do that, you can come in as soon as you're done."

"Okay..." she hesitates, "but I don't know how." Ever feel like that? God says "Do this," and we're like, *Uhh...* just like this kid.

So I say, "Grab the book right there. The skinny green one that says *Gardening With Vegetables*."

The child grabs three fat books in succession that do not say anything about vegetables or gardening, then declares the book isn't there.

I point to it for her. "That one. No, to the right. The *skinny* one, right there. It's green—no, lighter green...GARDENING WITH VEGETABLES, I said — yes, there you go." Good grief.

We both review the garlic section for thirty seconds. The child goes outside with instructions, a garlic bulb, and unveiled skepticism.

She returns two minutes later, declaring the ground is frozen, and requests to use Vin's shotgun to dig post holes for the garlic cloves. Alaska grown, I tell you.

Vin chimes in to remind her of the current temperature, and introduces her to the tool called "shovel."

Thirty minutes later, all the children start filtering back in the house, *right on time* (what do you know!) ...and I didn't have to plant the garlic.

In sum:

Gardening — check.

Homeschooling science lesson — check, check.

Parenting win — check.

I'll be in here knitting (and trying not to eat all the biscotti) if anyone needs anything else.

Help us, O Lord,
when we want to do the right thing,
but know not what it is.
But help us most when we know
perfectly well what we ought to do,
and do not want to do it.
Amen.

- Peter Marshall [3]

obedience laid bare

BY CYNTHIA HELLMAN

I've known the topic of this volume for a year. Writing this article has been the hardest, because I've been dragging my feet on another writing project (oh, the layers of irony in *that* sentence). Apparently, historical Christian fiction based on the woman who bled for twelve years doesn't write itself. Who knew?

As a writer (which I still struggle to call myself), it's intimidating to put my words out there for the world to see. There's a baring of my soul which is sometimes met with soft joy and reassurances, and sometimes with savage barbs —or worse yet, indifference from those whose opinions matter a great deal to me.

We all know what that's like though, don't we? You don't have to be a writer to know those feelings, amen? Introverts in a crowded room, a new mom who feels judgement for bottle feeding or going back to work, empty nesters who watch their children plummet headlong instead of soar out of the nest, the woman who miscarried again, or the one who faces the inquisition about why she prefers to not have children. Or how about this: being honest about your mental health struggles when you have no idea how it will be perceived, or stepping up to the podium or microphone to share what God has clearly called you to say, or seeking forgiveness when you know you were in the wrong. Ouch. Obedience has a way of peeling back the layers of our soul.

Let me say it a little louder for the people in the back row: Obedience requires vulnerability.

So, here it I sit, staring at the blinking cursor on my screen, praying for God to work through my paltry words. Books and website tabs lay open displaying Jewish culture, Capernaum temple sites, the average water temperature of the Sea of Galilee, and on and on it goes. That's when God whispers His truth and the grime of doubt washes away. *Dear one, I'm not asking for perfection; I'm asking for obedience. I'm asking for your widow's mite, not your surplus of average. I want what makes you you. I want the idiosyncrasies you wonder why on My green earth you possess. I want your deepest desires and most painful hurts. I want it all.*

It's when we lay our copper coins at the foot of the cross that His righteous touch lights up the rugged places of our soul. Holy pruning begins to take place, because we've placed ourselves at His mercy—we've chosen obedience over comfort, moving forward over shrinking back from what is Good in order to remain in what is known. God rarely allows warriors to play hopscotch on the sidelines while a battle rages; He mobilizes His people, and it begins with obedience.

We cannot hope to grow in obedience if we cannot be honest with ourselves, transparent with others, and laid bare before the Lord. But here's the really good part: God is good. He is so good, my friends. He cradles your obedience in the palm of His hand. He envelops you. He ushers you into His strong tower. Then He propels you toward His endless grace.

God is not an automaton, mindlessly accepting our obedience. He is woven through our stories because He is the author. Imagine that! An Author who doesn't struggle to call Himself what He is. I need to take a page from His playbook…or all the pages. He doesn't mind sharing His wisdom. So, I'll keep pounding out the story of a woman desperate for healing. We'll keep putting one foot in front of the other, shrugging on armor and testing the bonds of our shield of faith. It begins with my obedience. And yours.

stewards of the mysteries of God

By seven in the morning in September, the sky is just going from black to dark grey in our part of Alaska – and that morning, everyone else was still asleep. I, however, only had two and a half hours of sleep, and I felt pressure behind my eyes, on my scalp, and in my temples. And I felt so broken because everything seems like the end of the world when you're utterly exhausted and in pain. So I asked Him for a word.

And He gave me one, but it was for someone else. I texted it to her, and then listened again. Or, tried to listen. But frustrations kept coming to the surface and they wouldn't stay quiet – because, also when you're utterly exhausted and in pain, people are very irritating and those memories are very loud.

There was no word for me in that moment because the irritations were making too much noise. Or maybe there was a word, and it was to deal with those frustrations. Either way, in those early hours He walked me through praying forgiveness and we went through them, one by one.

Mostly it was me saying gracious-sounding things like, "I forgive so-and-so for being an idiot." And He understood; He knows I can be an idiot sometimes, too.

September is the new year that starts in the fall, and for most of us it is marked by change. New schools and classes, new routines, new places and friends and books and pencils. That month I also had two new doctors, a new email program, and some new projects I was working on…plus, also, my laptop made a ton of updates without asking me first (*I despise you, automatic updates*) so my computer files looked as unfamiliar as the ugly new dark mode on Facebook. So much change all at once.

All the newness can be exciting, but it's also stressful, yes? The change brings pressure to conform, to make things work out, or to make ourselves fit in. How much should we adapt? What does it mean for who we are, and what we do?

> *This is how one should regard us, as **servants of Christ** and **stewards of the mysteries of God**. Moreover, it is required of stewards that they be found faithful.*
>
> *- 1 Corinthians 4:1-2*

The paradox is that we change under pressure, but our identity is secure. Our value, standing, and purpose don't change. But as we become more like Him, we become more like ourselves – the person we were always meant to be.

And becoming that person requires stewardship.

We steward the pressure and change, and let it manifest as conviction: We stand firm in who He is – good, loving, faithful – in spite of circumstances that feel tenuous and shifty. And we stand firm in who we are – secure, learning, growing in patience and compassion, in spite of difficult situations and people who are inconsiderate, sinful, or intimidating.

> *But with me it is a very small thing that I should be judged by you or by any human court. In fact, I do not even judge myself.*
>
> *– 1 Corinthians 4:3*

When we hear the Lord's conviction about something, He will confirm it in various ways. **He wants us to hear Him.** He knows we want to get it right, and He, too, wants us to get it right – so when He convicts us, He's not playing tricks, being vague, or just talking to us in riddles. He will tell us something in several different ways because H*e wants us to hear* Him – and also because, yes, He knows we can be idiots sometimes.

If He calls us to make a big change and we are slow to pick up on it (or we need a lot of confirmation), He will allow us to get so uncomfortable with the status quo that the difficulties involved in making the change are less concerning than the reasons why that change needs to happen.

We cannot steward the mysteries of God if our agenda, our comfort zone, and our image are more important than what God is convicting us to do. We cannot steward the mysteries of God if we are bowing to pressure instead of conviction.

We cannot steward the mysteries of God if we are more concerned with looking right than doing right, and so become the unfaithful servant who was so afraid of the unknown that he hid his resources in the ground instead of stewarding them.

> *He also who had received the one talent came forward, saying, "Master, I knew you to be a hard man, reaping where you did not sow, and gathering where you scattered no seed,* **so I was afraid, and I went and hid your talent in the ground.** *Here you have what is yours.*
>
> - Matthew 25:24-25

Pressure feels like a tightness in your gut – you need to make a decision, or figure something out, or make something *just right*. Pressure feels like striving. But conviction is more like a fire in your belly to do what needs to be done at the earliest opportunity.

Pressure is, *God, what will they think?* But conviction is, *Lord, what do You think?*

Pressure is gas that bloats and inflates. Conviction is fire, bringing light and purity.

I'm familiar with pressure. The phone ringing, the baby crying, the pain searing, the decision fatigue. Only an hour left of the workday and still so much to do, and then the five-year-old starts banging on the piano. Pain and noise and time slipping and tasks looming. And I can't take it, I can't do it, it's all too much.

So He led me back to conviction and to stewardship. And as He will do, He immediately made me practice.

I sat down at the desk and wanted to write before anything else, to get the words out before I forgot them. But the words were about seeking Him first and He reminded me that I had not been in His Word yet, and this was my opportunity to live it out.

But I'll forget the words I need to write, I said.

I will cement them, He said.

And I opened the Bible to my bookmark in Deuteronomy, and wouldn't you know, it was right at the blessings of obedience. In case I wasn't paying attention, He was going to confirm His word with more words, but I would only hear it if I put things in the right order. If I

was too consumed with my own agenda and urgency, I'd miss it.

So I read a few verses, and they were good (blessings! Of course they were good!) and I thought of stopping there for the day so I could move on. Deadlines looming, you know.

But He said, *Do you really want to stop there? Is that where you want Me to stop, too? Or do you want the rest?*

Well, I want them all, of course. I don't want Him to stop. So I read the rest.

And the Lord will make you the head and not the tail, and you shall only go up and not down, if you obey the commandments of the Lord your God, which I command you today, being careful to do them, and if you do not turn aside from any of the words that I command you today, to the right hand or to the left, to go after other gods to serve them.

- Deuteronomy 28:13-14

And then He gave me the go ahead to start writing.

We steward the mysteries of God only when we hear Him more than anything or anyone else. It only happens when we focus on the fear of God instead of the fear of man. We cannot minister to others if we are not first and primarily ministering to the Lord.

(Are we in the Word every day? Are we praying and reading more than we're scrolling social media?)

We've got to let go of our agendas and comfort zones, our productions and planning – and I am a planner, so this is a whopper of a lesson for me, friends – and embrace those mysteries of God that force us to lean in and trust Him in the unknown.

...The rule of no realm is mine, neither of Gondor nor any other, great or small. But all worthy things that are in peril as the world now stands, those are my care. And for my part, I shall not wholly fail of my task, though Gondor should perish, if anything passes through this night that can still grow fair or bear fruit and flower again in days to come. **For I also am a steward.** *Did you not know?*

- J.R.R. Tolkien [4]

When we trust Him with those mysteries, He allows us to steward them. That looks like walking in freedom, love, truth, and boldness, in spite of pain or discomfort or what others might think. It looks like hearing His words for ourselves and others, and being moved to places we never could have gotten on our own.

When we do that, He will find us faithful, and we will see Him move in ways we never have before.

whatever it takes

BY RENEE PETTY

Go back to church, and your kids will sleep.

I remember vividly how angry His answer made me. I was exhausted, feeling alone, frustrated and desperate for help – my babies, now one and three, had never slept through the night at the same time. *God, please make my kids sleep.* And this is what He says to me? My response was venomous and defiant: *Make my kids sleep, and I will go back to church.* I remember this moment, because it was the moment I turned away from God. I loved Him all of my life, served Him, and in my darkest hour, His answer felt hollow and legalistic.

Looking back, I recognize my heart had been drifting toward this place for a long time. It was a hard season, one where all of the neatly stacked boxes of old wounds, insecurities, and lies I had believed were being knocked off the shelves of my heart, their contents spilling out. We always think we are so good at storing our junk, but eventually it overflows. I could not see it, but my heart had been slowly hardening, baby steps of disobedience and withdrawing from God, of allowing my perceptions and feelings to run amok. I did not arrive at turning away from God overnight, and it took many more months of going my own way before I would finally turn back toward Him.

I remember vividly, too, the moment I could see the destructive path I was on for what it was – sitting in my pastor's office, paralyzed by fear, sick in body and mind, desperate... again.

He leaned across the desk and said to me, *You are at a crossroads, Renee. You can continue to go your own way, or you can pursue Jesus in ways you have not ever done before. You get to choose.* I did not hesitate, I knew how incapable I was of sorting my own life. I needed Jesus. This time, I was going to listen; this time I was going to obey. *Whatever it takes, Lord, I will do it, I am done trying my own way.*

I would love to be able to tell you that when I made this decision to pursue God, to walk in obedience every day as best I could, that it was all peaches and sunflowers. But I cannot. It was a hard road plagued with self-doubt, fear, and the occasional pity party. God was, however, with me every step and together we left the Valley of Despair I had been living in. There were days I wanted to quit, to go back to what seemed the easier way, but I knew I could not. I had made my choice, *whatever it takes*. I learned of His faithfulness along the way and discovered just how deep His love for me is. I understood it was out of this love that He directed me. God is not a demanding task maker, desiring to see us jump through hoops for the sake of His own entertainment. God is a loving, merciful Father who sees what we cannot, who knows

what we cannot, and His direction is always for our good, not destruction. The more we understand the true nature and character of God, the easier obedience becomes.

Go back to church and your kids will sleep.

Turns out this wasn't a legalistic demand at all, but the key to healing the root of my children's restless nights. It wasn't lack of food or minerals that woke them up at night, or even bad genetics (my husband and I were not great sleepers). It was the palpable anxiety, depression, and fear I was living in every single day. When I let God in to begin healing my heart, He broke the stronghold of fear and my kids began to sleep. It's been years now, and I still have days I want to question God and the things He asks of me, but I choose to remember my babies, the work that He did, and I step forward into what He has for me. *Whatever it takes*, His way is better, always, and I can trust Him.

Blessed are the men of Noah's race that build
their little arks, though frail and poorly filled,
and steer through winds contrary towards a wraith,
a rumor of a harbor guessed by faith.

- J.R.R. Tolkien [5]

right of way

We were on the highway, driving out of town to a standard six-month checkup. We had passed the glittering fall days that are all steel and gold with leaves scattering the sidewalks; now we were onto the bare days, with smudged white skies and naked trees. They were empty, waiting. Most of the grass was bleached straw, but the grass around the streetlights was still fresh and green, like the oregano that grew up against our house. It clung to warmth and stayed steadfast long after the mint and plantain withered to nothing.

We had done this trip many times; it was our third year of these vision appointments. But this time our daughter could read, and yet out of one eye she could not see that the capital Y on the screen in front of her was a Y and not an O. The doctor changed the letter to an S, and she said it was an O. The doctor changed the sizes and arrangement of the letters, and the mood of this casual, standard appointment shifted to something weightier.

Remember what I've been telling you, Love, God said.

What He had been telling me was to thank Him in all things, even the hard things. Especially the hard things, those things that are a result of the Fall and not of Him at all. And He was teaching me that when I thank Him for those things, it wasn't as though I was saying, "Yes, this is so good, I'm glad (fill in the blank) has happened," as we would thank Him for, say, a windfall of cash or some unexpected victory.

It's a different kind of thankfulness. It feels like sacrifice.

When we thank Him for the hard things, we're saying, I *trust You. I know You're bigger than this, and as I trust and thank You in this, I am moving out of Your way and creating a wide path for You to move in power in this situation and use it for our great good.*

We are, in essence, giving God the right of way, and giving the enemy the middle finger.

The doctor changed the letter to a P and asked her what she saw. "O," she said.

She was a good reader and she knew her letters, but she couldn't see these. For the first time, he recommended therapy – twice a week, an hour long each time.

I knew it wasn't a big deal. Weekly appointments are not supposed to be a big deal. But it was a blow to a schedule already overwhelmed, and I was overwhelmed, and I didn't know how we were going to do this. I had been praying for breakthrough, not burden.

It wasn't cancer, it wasn't famine, it wasn't anyone attacking our village. It was just a new diagnosis and something else to add to the appointment book twice a week, and we were grateful that therapy was an option. I knew it was a first world problem. But we were first world people and I wanted my daughter to see.

Thank you, God.

I asked the doctor if the appointments could be only once a week. If we could do more at home. If there was any way we could avoid two appointments a week, anything to lighten this.

No, he said. Without therapy twice a week, he didn't think they could help her.

"I know this will be a challenge with your other responsibilities," he said. He knew we had six other kids, he knew some of them had special needs. And I was not going to cry in that chair, looking at that doctor and holding that baby and watching that daughter put her glasses back on.

Thank you, God.

He explained that insurance doesn't always cover the appointments, and that she needed them for six to nine months. He told me what they cost if we needed to pay out of pocket, and it was almost the same as our mortgage payment for each of those months.

Thank you, God.

I had never understood how praise could be a sacrifice, but I felt it then.

> *The one who offers thanksgiving as his sacrifice glorifies me;*
> *to one who orders his way rightly*
> *I will show the salvation of God!*
> *– Psalm 50:23*

He said that if she couldn't do therapy, the other option was surgery – which sometimes helps, and sometimes makes things worse. He didn't know we already had two surgeries in the last six months and another scheduled for the beginning of next year. And I was not going to cry in that office, holding that prescription and picking up my jacket and patting that baby.

Thank you, God.

Vince was waiting in the parking lot with the Stagecoach and the rest of the kids. I gave him the rundown and he suggested we get coffee. He is good at keeping things in perspective, and there are few adversities that caffeine and sugar can't help. But, I don't know, I kind of just wanted to go home and rave incoherently while tearing my schedule book into confetti.

> *Rejoice always, pray without ceasing, **give thanks in all circumstances;** for this is the will of God in Christ Jesus for you. Do not quench the Spirit.*
> *– 1 Thessalonians 5:16-19*

Notice the order? He tells us to not quench the Spirit right after he tells us to give thanks in everything. If not giving thanks smothers what the Spirit would do in our life, then giving thanks makes room for Him to light a fire under our sacrifice and sanctify our situation. We cling to warmth, trusting Him to keep us steadfast when we are tempted to wither. He blows the chaff away, like so many leaves in the fall.

> *God is in the midst of her; she shall not be moved;*
> *God will help her when morning dawns.*
> *– Psalm 46:5*

We coasted into downtown Wasilla when Vin broached the subject again. "If I can get over into the far right lane, we should stop at the coffee shop."

I looked at the traffic and assumed a somber Victorian accent. "We will leave it in the Lord's hands."

The little red car moved out of the way, and our Stagecoach merged into the lane. "Thus saith the Lord," he said, "Thou shalt have espresso."

I nodded. *Thank you, God.*

in between

BY JESSICA DASSOW

Four boys and one mom walked up the driveway to the storage shop, heat dissipating from the gravel and wildfire haze wafting in the air. We dug through dusty totes, found the ones we were looking for, and brandished them back down to the house. Smacking one a few times to relieve it of dust, I unzipped the large canvas duffle and began dispersing its contents upon a shady place on the ground.

"I miss the RV," our 15-year-old man-child remarked in his witty, deadpan, tongue-in-cheek way that we all love. A few chuckles erupted from our small crowd and we set to work, setting up the family tent for the first time since that man-child was a wee boy.

As we unfurled the tent, something sprayed out which made me catch my breath and my heart skip a beat. Immediately I was aware of the familiar, hollow space in my gut, which had lessened a bit but definitely hadn't dissipated like heat from gravel on this sultry, 95° day.

All this because of sand from Little Susitna riverbed. It had remained for all these years, tucked away in crawl spaces and moving vans and garages...and when those tiny fragments of my beloved homeland met my eyes, so did tears. It's amazing the love God can give for a place, so deep-seated that no matter where we find ourselves, it is carried along with us, like His presence.

So often we find ourselves in the in-between – that space from which we can still so easily look back with love and longing, and yet we can also strain to see ahead a place in life we are hoping for. Yet that future place can seem so out of reach. We miss what was, and we want what will be, and it feels somewhat paralyzing. Do we run back or do we move forward?

> *Let your eyes look directly forward, and your gaze be straight before you.*
> *– Proverbs 4:25*

We know we must move forward, so we pray and hope and muster up all our strength, and then realize it's not enough. So we go to the Wellspring and ask Him for more. He always says yes to us asking for more strength, but sometimes we tarry to move forward as we wonder why things just don't seem to be working out. Why our surroundings aren't right. Why relationships don't seem to be falling into place. Why we are plagued with so many annoyances. Why the job won't come. Why He isn't bringing healing. Why we just aren't settled.

We wonder about these things…we wonder if they ever will be. And it's so hard to be in this in-between, and to seek Him continually, and to continually hear, *You'll see. Be still, and know that I am God.*

> *Be still and know that I am God.*
> *– Psalm 46:10a*

Be still…when there seems to be no forward movement. Be still…when it all seems to be falling into place for everyone but you. Be still…as the number of fruitless job applications continue to mount. Be still…while your kids grow like wildfire and you feel desperate to be settled while they're all still home with you.

Be still. *Be still* doesn't mean to do nothing. It means to actively *know He is*. To be aware of His presence and sovereignty over all of your life and questions. To know and trust He's working it out and fighting battles, even ones which concern you and you know nothing about.

Sometimes moving forward feels like standing still. It can even feel backward. Sometimes despite abiding and being positioned to hear Him speak clearly, I hear nothing at all. I feel ready to do the thing, whatever it is, but there's no still, small voice, no open door, no baton being handed over...there seems to be nothing.

In these seemingly standstill times, we need brave obedience to do the last thing we heard Him tell us to do. Keep the holding pattern, a pilot would say. But unlike holding a flight pattern to wait your turn for a runway landing, in life we know the holding pattern can stretch to weeks to months to years in a confounding blur, leaving the faithful to wonder if they've missed something – missed a directive, opportunity, something.

> *I will instruct you and teach you in the way you should go; I will counsel you with my eye upon you.*
> – Psalm 32:8

That is the answer. When we abide and keep our eyes on Him, we won't miss anything. He'll make sure we hear. His eye is upon us; we can depend on Him to instruct, guide, and counsel us. While this is true, it's not so easy to put into practice. But consider that when we find ourselves "in-between," it is the most fertile ground for this lesson to grow.

It's easy to trust when things are going easily and smoothly. But when time goes on and we hit the real grit, will we "be still" then? Will we trust He has our best in mind...even when it doesn't match our dreams? When the forward motion seems to have lost momentum? When nothing makes sense and when the ground seems fallow?

That ground we spread our tent upon was in dire need of landscaping. Of any sort of green. So after the snow said farewell in the spring, we chose one small section and began hauling rocks out, load by load. We dug out dead shrubs. Placed edging to provide boundaries for the new green growth we hoped for. We spread a load of soil, and we seeded and watered. And then we hoped, for two days anyway, until a massive, freak storm moved in and all our hard work careened down the driveway in torrents of rain.

We reseeded, and began watering many times per day to keep up with the sweltering heat. Days became weeks. Nothing grew.

Our son stared at the ground one day, then broke the silence with, "I'm really beginning to resent this yard project. It won't grow....like anything here...it's just so hard." Would we quit or move forward?

We went through and tediously pulled all the weeds that had sprung up. Hoed up the compacted soil that the hard rain had beat down. Replaced the peat the torrents had washed away. Reseeded and applied new seedling fertilizer. With hope, we began watering again, during the very hottest part of the summer. And you know what? With much time, diligent watering and weeding, and subsequent seeding, it was growing. Finally we could see the momentum building. And it was beautiful.

We're being tended like this, and so much more diligently and tenderly, by the Gardener. He knows the boundaries we need for this present time. Much is happening as we take our sometimes small but significant steps forward. He is breaking up our hard places. He is sowing and nurturing. When the storms come and the lack of our strength is revealed, He is patiently reseeding. We're in His good care, and though we aren't readily seeing growth, it is there, if only hidden in tiny seeds beneath the surface of fertile soil – the fertile soil of the "in-between" where brave obedience to move forward is required and grown.

An adventure is only
an inconvenience rightly considered.
An inconvenience is only
an adventure wrongly considered. [6]

The Christian ideal has not been tried
and found wanting.
It has been found difficult,
and left untried. [7]

— G.K. Chesterton

How it's going around here:
- Think about the next project.
- Decide on step 1 for the next project.
- Realize that step 1 requires stepping away from the chips and salsa to type with two hands.
- Continue eating chips and salsa.

We almost had our first snow that day, so we almost put on Christmas music. Instead, we worked like normal – except for when I didn't work at all and answered a phone call from a friend whom I hadn't talked to in forever. And then, since I was already making those kinds of carpe diem choices (and also because everyone else was out of the house and I wasn't supervised) I ate pecan pie for lunch.

But after that, I finally put in a few hours of actual work. When I came back down to the kitchen, I discovered one of the kids had baked cinnamon clove raisin bread, encrusted with sugar on the top. And suddenly I found myself so far off the no-sugar wagon that I may as well have laid down and let the stupid thing drive over me repeatedly, back and forth, until January.

I don't know if you know this, but writers are notorious for procrastinating, and snacking is one of our favorite ways to do it. It takes discipline to sit at the desk, stay in the chair, stare at the screen, and tap the words out. And sometimes I don't have it in me.

But I do have a list of things that need to be done, and I want to move forward in them. But it takes persistence. It takes turning off social media. It takes hard thinking. It takes choosing obedience over ease and distraction.

All it really takes is doing.

> *Those who forever seek the will of God are overrun by those who do it.*
> – Reinhard Bonnke

At the end of the week I used to ask myself, "Did I do enough?" The answer was always no. Or, maybe not no, exactly, but it never felt like I could answer *yes* with a clear conscience because there was always so much more that needed to be done. It wasn't a fair question, even when I didn't spend egregious amounts of time staring at the computer screen while eating chips and salsa, wishing I had a third hand to type with.

Now, though, I ask myself this question: "Did I end the week strong?" It's still not an easy one to answer when your work is mostly intangible things. But it is, at least, a fair question. Sometimes I feel pretty good about it, and other times I don't. When I don't feel good about it, I feel frustrated – or worse, like I failed.

So for wholeness' sake, let's break down what "ending strong" means:

- Did I accomplish what realistically had to be done, in light of the inevitable chaos and interruptions throughout the week? Did I make forward progress, even if it's not as far as I wanted to go?
- Am I able to look back at that chaos and those interruptions without resentment toward myself or others? (If not, do not pass Go, do not collect $200, but immediately walk through forgiveness and prayer. No messing around. Our joy is at stake in this.)

For me, those two criteria are the bottom line. I could measure or quantify a lot of things, but in this season, numbers are not the priority.

Relationships are the priority.
Wholeness is the priority.
Forward progress is the priority.
Abiding is the priority.

And keeping those things in mind is how we start the next week strong, too.

Another question that helps me stay on track is this one: *God, how do I seek Your kingdom right now, in this moment?* When I am making dinner. When I am talking to my kids. When I'm scrolling social media. When I'm working at my desk. When I'm gathering socks and toys and books and a million things throughout the living room that need to be put away.

> *But seek first the kingdom of God and his righteousness, and all these things will be added to you.*
> *— Matthew 6:33*

And He answers in different ways. Sometimes it's to clean up after myself better. Sometimes He tells me to stop talking and listen more. Often He tells me to turn off the phone. And sometimes He says to leave the toys and everything alone, and make the kids clean them up.

But whatever it is, the answer comes as a result of abiding. Recognizing He is right there is the root to any Kingdom-seeking. It has to happen first.

The next day was Saturday. I was under a blanket, and Dash, the 24-toed cat, was on top of it. It was a quiet afternoon and most of the kids were outside, one was napping on my bed, afternoon coffee was almost ready, and books were piled on the bench in front of me. My goals list was on top of the stack. And He was right there, closer than Dash.

But earlier, when it was not so perfect, He was there, too.

He was there when the toddler was crawling all over me, all elbows and knees and bruises.

He was there when the kids were arguing and I threatened extra chores.

And He'll be there later, when it's bedtime and jammies and brushing teeth and prayer and seven kids in a hundred directions and so much noise you'd never believe we were trying to convince them it's almost time to be unconscious.

But in that moment of the afternoon, the kids were coming in and blowing their noses from playing in fresh snow. We shushed them so they wouldn't wake the baby; candles were lit and lamps were on and the sun had set at least thirty minutes earlier.

He was right there, as close as the goals list, which I looked at the same way Dash was looking at a magpie out the window – slightly alarmed, but planning to eat that thing for lunch. On it was books to read and people to contact, projects to finish and projects to begin. Pages to edit, and pages to write. All it takes is doing.

And He said, *Get off the phone, Love. Grab your books. This nap won't last forever.*

AMERICAN POETRY
DE MILLE
The PATH to HOME WHEN DAY IS DONE
Guest

an evening prayer for bold obedience

Dear God,
Unify Your people,
Comfort Your people,
Grow and mature Your people.
And help them avoid the spirit of stupid on social media.
Amen.

Not everyone has to agree with you or like you. In fact, in the current culture, if everyone agrees with you and likes you, you're probably either compromising some of your values or succumbing to intimidation about being silent about those values.

Your beliefs matter. Truth matters. Listening matters. And standing up to people who project otherwise matters.

This is not a time for Christians to go silent and mistake turning the other cheek for being a doormat. The Bride needs to stop acting like popular culture is her abusive, domineering boyfriend, and remember Whose she is.

She is — you are — loved, valued, and known by the King. She is — and you are — worth protecting and standing up for.

We're not keeping the peace when the Lord tells us to speak but we bow to the fear of man and stay silent.

We're not keeping the peace when God tells us to act but we stay on the sideline.

If we worship the approval of others more than God, we are like Gomer in the book of Hosea. (Not sure who that is? Short book, good reading. Spoiler alert: She's not a role model.)

We're meant to live free, and where the Spirit of the Lord is, there is freedom.[8] It's worth standing up for.

> *For you were called to freedom, brothers. Only do not use your freedom as an opportunity for the flesh, but through love serve one another. For the whole law is fulfilled in one word: "You shall love your neighbor as yourself." But if you bite and devour one another, watch out that you are not consumed by one another.*
>
> *- Galatians 5:13-15*

Our loyalties are revealed by our obedience: Do we fear God and worship Him, or do we fear man and worship ourselves?

With the right answer, we can go to sleep in peace. We can wake up in peace, unafraid and unintimidated. We can stand for truth, without throwing pearls to swine or arguing with the spirit of stupid. We can just walk in love and... #blesstheirhearts.

apple snug

I am not sure how I stumbled on this, but during one of my many forays into gluten-free, sugarless eating I discovered that sautéed apples are good, but sautéed apples with nuts and feta are a million times better. Now it's my fall go-to for breakfast, lunch, and midnight snack.

This recipe can be multiplied as many times as you need (1 apple equals approximately 1 serving) to feed a crowd.

ingredients:
1 apple, diced
¼ cup walnuts and/or pecans, coarsely chopped
2-3 tablespoons of feta, goat cheese, or blue cheese
1 tsp. butter
cinnamon

1. Melt the butter in the pan and sauté the apples on medium-low, stirring every couple of minutes – you don't want them to scorch, but you do want to give them time to sear and caramelize a little.

2. When the apples are just starting to do that, toss in the chopped nuts. Turn the heat to low and cook for 2-3 minutes longer, stirring frequently.

3. Scrape the cooked apples and nuts into a bowl and crumble feta (or other stinky cheese of your choice) on top. Add a shake or three of cinnamon on top and enjoy.

pumpkin spice scones with cardamom icing

BY MĒGAN ANCHETA
makes 10-12

Fall is one of my favorite times of year, and pumpkin-spiced treats like these are just one small reason why. These scones are perfect paired with a cup of tea or coffee.

ingredients:
1 cup sorghum flour
1/2 cup millet flour or brown rice flour
1/2 cup tapioca flour
1/3 cup brown sugar
1 tablespoon baking powder
3/4 teaspoon xanthan gum
3/4 teaspoon cinnamon
1/2 teaspoon nutmeg
1/2 teaspoon ginger
1/2 teaspoon ground cloves
1/2 teaspoon sea salt
1/2 cup palm shortening
1/2 cup unsweetened pumpkin puree
3-4 tablespoons hemp milk
2 teaspoons vanilla extract
1 large egg

1. Preheat oven to 425 degrees (F) and line a baking sheet with parchment paper or a silicone liner.

2. In a large mixing bowl, whisk together the dry ingredients. Cut in the shortening until mixture resembles coarse crumbs.

3. In a small mixing bowl, whisk together pumpkin, hemp milk, vanilla, and egg. Pour the wet mixture into the dry and mix until just combined.

4 Using an ice cream scooper, scoop the dough into balls and place on the prepared baking sheet. Wet your fingers and carefully pat down the tops of the dough balls until the dough is 3/4 to 1-inch thick.

5 Bake for 11 - 13 minutes. The scones will not be visibly brown when finished baking; however, the bottom of the scones should be light golden brown when done. Do not over bake.

6 Allow to cool completely on cooling racks before icing.

cardamom icing

ingredients:
3/4 cup organic powdered sugar
3-5 teaspoons hemp milk
Pinch of cardamom (a very small pinch... a little goes a long way)

Whisk together ingredients until smooth and add milk until icing reaches desired consistency.

Drizzle on cooled scones.

proximity:
where brokenness becomes wholeness

I had spent much of the day standing up to a kid who kept trying to steamroll me, trying to ram through the line I was holding. At least six times that day, in so many words, I had said, "Here's a boundary, kid. Learn to use it."

And then when it was finally calm and quiet enough for me to hear my own thoughts, I sat down and opened the Word, and read this:

> O Jerusalem, Jerusalem, the city that kills the prophets and stones those who are sent to it! How often would I have gathered your children together as a hen gathers her brood under her wings, and you were not willing!
>
> – Matthew 23:37

He longed to gather them and they refused, choosing to keep Him at a safe distance with their own rebellion. And I was reminded again that Jesus knows what it's like – far more than I do – to be the parent of hard kids. He knows more than I do what it's like to hold it together when it would be easier to lash out, and to persist in loving the hard person and doing the hard thing when you'd rather throw in the towel.

He gets it. He gets us, right where we're at, in all of our coffee-chugging, gritty-loving, expletive-repressing, deep-breathing glory. He is right here with us.

> *... a bruised reed he will not break, and a smoldering wick he will not quench, until he brings justice to victory; and in his name the Gentiles will hope.*
>
> - Matthew 12:20-21

Hurting people hurt people. We know that, right? It takes a ton of maturity, wisdom, and grace to rise above it. Our own wounds are often triggered by someone else acting out of their wounds, and if we don't deal with our own brokenness, we're likely to lower ourselves to the level of someone else's behavior. Until we accept responsibility for our own stuff, we'll have a hard time accurately discerning the difference between God's plan for us versus the enemy's attempts to manipulate us.

None of us are entitled to play the double

standard in wounding others. It might be tempting to use our background as an excuse, but our experience and expertise are platforms for compassion, not entitlement. This is what separates people who lead from people who are just narcissists looking for a fan club. When we walk in wholeness we can bend low, dig deep, and rise above.

But lookee here, friends:

> *He did not speak to them without a parable, but privately to his own disciples He explained everything.*
>
> - Mark 4:34

Proximity equals privilege. Closeness, intimacy, and time spent with Him equals favor, revelation, and understanding, and sometimes our broken places find healing faster than we could have imagined when we bring them to Him. This is why we abide: it changes our days, and then it changes our lives, and then it changes the lives around us.

Anyone can give up; it takes nothing at all to throw up your hands and say, *That's it, I'm done, c'est la vie, it's just not worth it and I don't care enough anymore.* But it takes holy stubbornness to stay steadfast, unshrinking, pursuing what He's called you to until the fight is over and you've finished the work He called you to. And sometimes, that work is within us.

Your most powerful achievement might be what you most want to shrink back from. So...don't. He is eager to hear you and speak to you. He doesn't speak in riddles, play tricks or wait for us to make a mistake so He can pounce on us. He's right here with us, in the middle of all our moments, waiting to reveal the Kingdom to us.

So, a word for big brave you – doing the hard thing, the patient thing, the gentle thing when you'd rather just break something: He is cheering you on in your steadfastness. You aren't investing in thin air, you are doing something wise and wonderful, accomplishing great things. Holy stubbornness equals eternal reward.

Our brokenness brought to Jesus equals wholeness.

We're living in a time of eager expectation to see the fruit that comes from people who boldly deal with their past, because they are the ones who will walk shamelessly into a future bigger than they ever dared to imagine.

...be *steadfast*, immovable, always *abounding* in the work of the Lord, knowing that in the Lord your *labor* is not in vain.

— 1 corinthians 15:58

study guide

This flexible, light-yoked guide is for you to use on your own or with a small group. We've included questions to use for personal journaling or group discussion, scripture to study, copy down, and memorize, and short prompts for prayer. It's not homework or another thing to add to your list – it's just movement forward and rest for your soul, friends.

move me

questions

What do I need motivation for right now?

What is keeping me from moving?

What would make me really want to move in that thing? And what will I do about it?

scripture

Acts 17:26-31

prayer

Lord, thank You for letting me partner with You in work that You have designed for me. Help me to honor that partnership, and to not hesitate when You've made the next step clear.

mountain climbers and obedience

questions

When thinking of obedience, do I think of it as being for my benefit?

When was the last time I hesitated to obey? Why?

When have I found myself in a place or position better then I could have imagined?

scripture

Ephesians 3:20

prayer

Heavenly Father, I ask You to shift my perspective on obedience. Allow me to see it as something exciting and as beneficial to me. Reveal to me the areas that I don't trust your goodness and carefulness towards me.

carrying fire

questions

How am I currently carrying fire in my life?

Am I extinguishing fire in a different area that He's called me to obey in? How is this working against what I want for my life?

What would it look like if I wasn't afraid of getting burned?

scripture

Jeremiah 9:23-24

prayer

Lord, I want to go and do and obey. I want to set my agenda aside and move in Your ways. I repent of smothering my own growth. Help me to hear You clearly and be bold in moving forward.

following instructions

questions

What breakthrough am I currently waiting for?

How can I rejoice in advance?

scripture

1 Thessalonians 5:16-24

prayer

God, You are good and I can trust You. Give me a greater vision for what You want to do in the situations I'm praying for. Thank You for moving in all the ways I cannot see.

obedience laid bare

questions

How does obedience feel vulnerable to me right now?

How will my obedience encourage others around me?

Where is God mobilizing me in this season?

scripture

Luke 8:40-48

prayer

Holy Spirit, help me to be honest with myself and with You as I walk in vulnerable obedience. I want to grow in the grace You have for me and partner with You in ways that expand the Kingdom.

stewards of the mysteries of God

questions

How has God been confirming the direction He wants me to move in?

Am I bowing to pressure lately, or moving in conviction? How can I tell?

How can I practice conviction and stewardship in the situation He is leading me in right now?

scripture

1 Corinthians 4

prayer

Lord, help me to hear Your words more than anyone or anything else so I can walk in the ways You've set before me. Thank You for speaking. Thank You for teaching me to recognize Your voice, and for moving me to places I never could have gotten to on my own.

whatever it takes

questions

Is there a hard situation where I am still insisting on my own agenda?

What is God offering instead?

What can I do today, and this week, to move toward that?

scripture

1 Corinthians 1:18-21

prayer

Jesus, I know I am incapable of sorting out my own life. I need Your help and wisdom to walk in freedom, peace, and wholeness. Thank You for always offering those to me, for being patient with me, and for teaching me to let go of my own agenda.

right of way

questions

What do I need to thank God for right now that feels like a sacrifice?

What might it look like for God to light a fire under my sacrifice and sanctify my situation?

scripture

Psalm 46, Romans 8:28

prayer

Lord, thank You for moving in this situation. Help me to be steadfast and stay out of Your way so it will go according to Your plan and not according to my fears. I know You can bring good out of this that I never could have imagined.

in between

questions

In what areas of my life do I find myself in the "in between?"

How will I allow these areas to become fertile ground for growth in brave obedience to move forward?

How do I see God tending to me in this season?

scripture

Philippians 3:12-15, Isaiah 43:18-19

prayer

Father, thank You that Your eye is upon me. You give me the direction and guidance I need at just the times I need it. Help me to "be still" and trust You are working all things for my good and for Your glory, even when it feels like I'm standing still or going backwards. Help me to have courage to obey You and move forward confidently, however small the steps.

all it takes is doing

questions

What are my priorities in this season?

How can I evaluate my progress based on those?

What helps me choose obedience over ease and distraction?

scripture

Matthew 6:25-34

prayer

Jesus, help me to not be too hard or too soft on myself. Help me to seek Your Kingdom in all the moments and to remember that You are with me, available in every moment as I need Your wisdom and perspective and motivation. Thank You for helping me do what needs to be done.

an evening prayer for bold obedience

questions

Is there any area in my life where I have been fearing man more than God?

Is there any area where I am more concerned with pleasing others than pleasing God?

How is God calling me to walk in both unity and boldness right now?

scripture

Acts 4:23-31

prayer

Lord, help me to be more concerned with what You think than what others think. Help me to speak when you call me to and to not shrink back, and help me to know when to be silent. Thank You for giving me peace and composure when You call me to bold things, and for making it easier to walk in boldness and love the more I practice it.

proximity

questions

Do I tend to lower myself to the level of anyone else's behavior? What wound is behind this that still needs healing?

What experience and background do I have (either positive or negative) that God wants to use for compassion toward others, instead of entitlement?

What am I wanting to shrink back from? What might God want to do with that situation, instead?

scripture

Mark 4:30-34

prayer

Holy Spirit, thank You for making wholeness out of my brokenness and using it for Your Glory. Reveal anything to me that needs to be addressed, and help me to do the work of healing in my own heart so I can help others walk in healing and victory, too.

notes

1. For "In him we live and move and have our being; as even some of your own poets have said, "For we are indeed his offspring." (Acts 17:28)

2. Rejoice always, pray without ceasing, give thanks in all circumstances; for this is the will of God in Christ Jesus for you. (1 Thessalonians 5:16-18)

3. Peter Marshall, Prayer to the U.S. Senate, February 2, 1948.

4. J.R.R. Tolkien, *Return of the King*, (Boston: Houghton Mifflin Company, 1993), 30.

5. J.R.R. Tolkien, "Mythopoeia," http://www.tolkien.ro/text/JRR%20Tolkien%20-%20Mythopoeia.pdf.

6. G.K. Chesterton, "On Running After Ones Hat," *All Things Considered*, Project Gutenberg, https://www.gutenberg.org/files/11505/11505-h/11505-h.htm.

7. G.K. Chesterton, *What's Wrong with the World*, Project Gutenberg, https://www.gutenberg.org/files/1717/1717-h/1717-h.htm.

8. *Now the Lord is the Spirit, and where the Spirit of the Lord is, there is freedom.* (2 Corinthians 3:17)

also by shannon guerra

the Work That God Sees series
prayerful motherhood in the midst of the overwhelm

Moms, you pour yourselves out every day. How about some powerful refilling, in small, easy doses?

Short chapters. White space. Deep down hope, and out loud laughter. Because you have what it takes. You are watched over and known by the God who notices every detail, and He meets you in these mundane moments and is breathing them into mighty movement.

Work That God Sees is available as six individual little books, or as a complete, all-in-one edition with the content from all six books (including the snarky recipes, crafty patterns, and questions for personal journaling or small group discussion) plus 25 pages of extra stories, recipes, and lessons you can learn at someone else's expense.

Oh My Soul

encountering God in honest, unconventional (and sometimes messy) prayer

What if there was **one thing** you could do that would always, without fail, make you more **whole** and **healed** and **at peace** than you were the day before...would you do it?

What if, at the same time, that one thing transformed the world around you?

This is what happens when we encounter God, living in His presence, in continual conversation with Him.

We want to hear God better, and to know His will for all the messy, mundane details of our life. But does He still speak to us when we are distracted, grumpy, overwhelmed, and unprepared?

How can we have "quiet time" with God when there's no quiet, and no time? Can we really know the will of God and move forward in obedience, in spite of our fears and failures?

And, if we're really honest with Him, will He strike us with lightning? Or will we end up praying with boldness and authenticity like never before?

Available as the original book, companion journal, and 21-day devotional study.

upside down

understanding and supporting attachment in adoptive and foster families

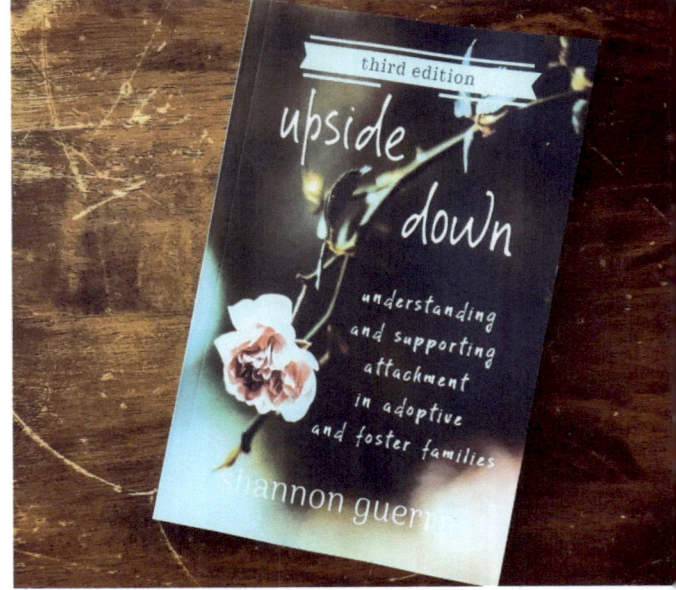

This book gives hope to adoptive and foster families, and the lowdown for those who love them.

Adoptive and foster families working through attachment issues often feel alone, but their communities can intentionally be part of the solution instead of unintentionally being part of the problem. Without that support, adoptive and foster families live in isolation.

Shannon Guerra learned this firsthand after she and her husband adopted two of their children in 2012. She started writing shockingly transparent blog posts about what her family was going through at home, at the doctor's office, and in her heart as a mama.

And then adoptive and foster families started writing back.

Their overwhelming, unanimous theme was, **"This is what I've wanted to tell people for so long. I wish everyone who knows our family could read this."**

This book is the result. In about 100 pages, *Upside Down* provides information and insight that transforms an outsider's assumptions into an insider's powerful perspective. Because adoptive and foster families should never feel alone, and our communities can be equipped to make sure they never feel that way again.

the ABIDE series
a year of growing deep + wide

volume titles:

rest in the running

hope in the waiting

clarity in the longing

bravery for the next step

obedience to move forward

surrendering to win

ABIDE is off the beaten path: A 6-volume series of fully illustrated books that are part devotional, part coffee table book, part magazine. These six beautiful books will lead you further into the presence of God as you grow deep and wide, pressing forward in these seasons that stretch us. Each book contains full color photographs, a light-yoked study section for personal or small group use, an extra recipe or two, and powerful encouragement that meets you where you're at and moves you forward.

one more thing...

Need a little white space in the chaos?

You are warmly invited to copperlightwood.com, where we're transparent about finding peace in the hard moments and beauty in the mess. I hope you'll hit the subscribe button and poke around all the posts and videos. Just keep in mind that it's a little unpolished here, so watch out for the Legos on the floor.

Bless you, friend,
Shannon Guerra

connect:
gab: shannonguerra
mewe: shannonguerra
telegram: Shannon Guerra
clouthub: shannonguerra
goodreads: shannonguerra
pinterest: copperlightwood

email:
shannon@copperlightwood.com

www.ingramcontent.com/pod-product-compliance
Lightning Source LLC
Chambersburg PA
CBHW042257100526
44589CB00003B/54